Life is a Stage

Lita Rosén

BookLeaf Publishing

Presentation by *BookLeaf Publishing*

Web: www.bookleafpub.com

E-mail: info@bookleafpub.com

ISBN: 9789357213431

First edition 2023

First Light

Swimmingly, is how my life began;
More literally than you might think;
Nestled in my Mothers' abdomen;
With no idea where I may end;
UK, Russia; France or Kazakhstan?

I felt myself begin to shift;
Prepared to fall or fly;
Into the blinding mist;
Soar into a utopia;
Or plunge into an unforgiving abyss.
My internal safety gone in an instant;

A scream tore through my new lungs;
Proving I was existent;
With flailing limbs, crying eyes;
And perfectly working pistons.

Everything was unknown;
Yet the arms that held me;
Safe, very much like home;
One look into the woman's eyes;
Told me I'd never be alone.

I forced a smile onto my face;

Through the crust and blood;
I knew of our shared fates;
The tearful woman was my Mother;
With whom I was embraced.

There was an entire world to explore;
Something entirely anew;
Fountains of knowledge to scour;
Love, hate and despair to feel;
All upon this floating sphere;
With that freedom, I was blessed;
From my first breath of air.

Guardian's Lesson

My knees scraped against;
The carpet, remaining upbeat;
Though one thing I sensed;
This world was full of feet!

Red heels, black Spatz, white pumps;
Trod into my path;
The adults had gather in clumps;
Huddled, heads bowed as in mass;
Disco-ordination caused some bumps.

A friendly man knelt on the floor;
My Grandfather, with sparkling eyes;
A man that I now loved more and more;
Like my heart had tripled in size;
So much, he was one that I adored.

He lifted me into his arms;
And my heart soared;
Well versed in charms;
More treasured than a dragon's hoard;
Was that man in smart garms.

At least, for myself;
There was no-one or nothing;
More important on my shelf;
And certainly, I was no more doting;

Than to that mischievous elf.

He made me feel wanted and important;
Granddad with his wicked jokes;
His teasing may have been constant;
But he was far better than most folks;
No matter how hard you'd hunt.

Then appeared my Grandma in red shoes;
Her favourite colour, of course;
Than her spouse, she was less easy to amuse;
And spoke with a little more force;
Though a never-ending fuse.

Much needed for such pranks;
As Granddad was known to pull;
Though never high in the ranks;
T'was the Captain of never being dull;
For which he had my thanks.

I had many more too;
For my Grandmother also;
For the many things she knew;
About clothes, life, and more thorough;
Though then, I had no clue;
As I learnt with my mouth solo.

My mother and her parents, I adored;
But my father was another matter;
Mostly, he was one I abhorred;
Him, I never did flatter;

His insults often left me floored.

At that age, I didn't understand;
But it wouldn't take me long;
Snatched from the arms of a gentler man;
The end of my happy song;
A girl separated from her clan.

At that point, I cried;
I soon knew that was a mistake;
As no matter how I tried;
He'd always forced me to break;
Every time he lied.

I still had much to discover;
About people, interactions and words;
Body language and more to cover;
Things both normal and absurd;
Over many topics, I would hover.

But first of all, before that starts;
The joy of being young should prevail;
Though my childhood, by carts;
Would be halted and potentially fail;
The magic punctured by darts;
And enthusiasm curtailed.

A Child’s Best Friend

Stumbles, bumps, scrapes and tumbles;
Accompanied by giggles and falls;
Sometimes squeals and mumbles;
For whatever the occasion calls;
Frolics through the grass, or rolling through brambles.

Upon my childhood adventures;
I took along my best friend;
An old dog requiring dentures;
Who’d follow me to the bitter end;
And was never one of the backbenchers.

They were always by my side;
And kept me out of mischief;
My love for them would not subside;
No greater treasure in the Barrier Reef;
And none in which I’d rather confide.

Upon our path, I went a cropper;
Grazed my knees something fierce;
Though the blood would fit in a dropper;
It felt like a deadly pierce;
That’d got me good and proper.

My canine friend attended;
To my ‘grave’ injuries;
Didn’t want them to be offended;
But their licks in flurries;
Made me, in my pain, suspended.

I admit, I tried it once myself;
To see if it would help;
But the taste of blood itself;
Made me gag and yelp;
I put that idea back on the shelf!

In some ways, I’d have rather have been a dog;
Human responsibilities and chores;
Didn’t want to be in my log;
Hidden behind large oak doors;
It would have been so much better to be a dog!

I’d soon learn I was wrong;
The sad thing about dogs;
Is they don’t live very long;
A sorrow I accompanied with sobs;
For they should live ever-long.

Hellish (?) Education

Every child had that time;
When they have to abandon play;
For activities as sour as a lime;
Disgusting in every way;
With no apparent reason or rhyme.

I couldn't even bring my ally;
They had to be left at home;
A part of me hoped time would fly;
So I wouldn't feel so alone;
And my mouth so painfully dry.

My stomach was in knots;
With both excitement and fear;
As it churned and gargled lots;
I held my mother near;
So that she would forget me, not.

I dragged my feet;
All the way there;
That place I'd meet;
My end, I swear!
My life too short to be complete.

We arrived at the foreboding gate;

My hand gripped Mother's tight;
I was sure I'd hate;
Whatever was inside;
Which was sure to seal my fate.

I turned to mother;
And looked at her with pleading eyes;
She said: "It's not a bother;
Soon, it'll be home time."
I was sure that – of school – I'd never be a lover.

It took me away from my toys;
From playing and making stories;
I had to deal with smelly boys;
Definitely one of the lesser glories;
Though – I was told – when I'd get older, they'd be joys?

My arms remained folded;
Whilst I was forced into the yard;
I was sure to have been scolded;
If I had made a run for the car;
And well-and-truly bolted.

The witchy teacher sneered;
Like a hungry bird of prey;
When I walked past, she leered;
As though she'd eat me where I lay;
Or something similar, I feared.

She smiled and waved to me;
I simply narrowed my eyes;
I didn't appreciate false sincerity;
Those poorly veiled lies;
Only gave me animosity.

Although, once inside, it wasn't the torture I'd imagined;
Quiet children sat at tables;
Bright colours and artsy designs, it so happened;
Littered the walls – not as I had fabled;
My ornate fears seemingly flattened.

There were letters and numbers;
Stories and worlds to explore;
Despite my previous blunders;
I just want to learn, I'd implore;
My teachers' knowledge, I would plunder.

She was even seen in a new light;
Not evil, or a child eater,
Not an angel either – in the middle – just right;
For the next day, I was bizarrely eager;
But that would come with the morning light;

For now, I was just happy to go back;
To my canine playmate;
And my favourite building block stack;
I hoped I wouldn't be home too late;

My tummy growled for a snack.

I ran to my mother for a hug;
Much like old Honey did to myself;
Once I stepped onto our hall's rug;
With a love of extraordinary wealth;
Imagine the amount I felt like a mug;
When I knew I had to go near everyday until
year twelve?!

Unexpected Friend

It became increasingly evident;
That it was difficult to survive;
In any school environment;
Without human friends with drive;
Though the majority were… Inclement.

They were either too smart;
Or lacking in the brains to understand any
intellect;
Some had a manner far too tart;
Whilst others already had their own sect;
I didn't know where to start;

I'd always been happy in my own company;
Albeit for Honey and my Grandparents;
My mother thought my comments were funny;
Of social skills with peers, there was no
evidence;
It would be something of an anomaly.

They all seemed to eye me strangely;
Like I had two heads;
Was I somehow quite ungainly?
Or perhaps sewn from loose threads;
And wandered lamely?

I also wouldn't know what to say;
If I was forced to;
How did I talk to people of my age?
It wasn't something I had planned to do;
T'wasn't written on my page.

Then, as if by magic;
A peer approached me, with a smile;
I was sure this was to be tragic;
Socialising wasn't my style;
But it appeared I had a power, kinetic.

They didn't stop coming forward;
With eyes of intent;
Please, don't think me a coward;
But I started to feel contempt;
For the one I'd seemingly collared.

The way they approached;
With reckless abandon;
I wish I'd have been coached;
As that someone who had a hand in;
My privacy being encroached.

I cowered and was internally concerned;
Why had they taken an interest in me?
This was clearly a confidence that had to be learned;
A power I could never see;

Being within myself 'til it burned.

The child opposite giggled with glee;
Then asked for my name;
It sprung from me;
As though blurting a rude word again;
Another thing for which I gained a penalty.

They seemed to rather enjoy it;
That odd little alien in my sight;
It seemed to give them some sort of benefit;
To see me wound so tight;
Quite frankly, it was somewhat sick.

Then, they explained who they were;
With disturbing enthusiasm;
Their words came out as a babbled slur;
Executed without elocution;
And with hands waved in the air.

Despite my complaining;
I was grateful they had introduced themselves;
Forced socialising was draining;
But never when it was us elves;
It was a friendship worth maintaining.

Even into adulthood;
You remained a close friend;
The test of time, our friendship withstood;

In fact, until your end;
The girl enthusiastic for sisterhood;
Was – to me – the perfect blend;
Of crazy, and someone who understood.

Demons Are Here

Whilst I had one friend;
Weird, unparalleled and bizarre;
There were far more that had dislike as a trend;
And sometimes, they took it too far;
It seemed as though it'd never end.

But I knew how to take it;
I had a 'coping' mechanism;
Something that seemed fit;
When attacked on a prism;
By those so dimly lit.

I felt the punches land;
Upon my tender flesh;
It made it hard to stand;
As I saw less and less;
I blocked out more than I had planned.

My consciousness started to wain;
Whilst a kick thumped my stomach;
Calm and silence difficult to maintain;
My body was completely flummoxed;
And my collar gained a bloodstain.

A teacher finally intervened;
After I had been made mincemeat of;
Her face almost seemed serene;
Not like someone who would give a telling off;
But, how much had she seen?

I was only eleven;
Naïve and tried to only see the best;
Had I been more cynical then;
Kept my heart closer to my chest;
I might not have been hurt by those men…

Enough of the ifs and buts;
The past is what it is;
At that time, I was in a rut;
Bombarded by a harsh chorus;
That never seemed to let up.

They sat me in an not-so-comfy chair;
Once I was in sick bay;
With blood and spit clogging my hair;
There was nothing I could say;
I did nought but stare.

T'was what I did at home;
When my father started;
He shouted at I alone;
His intimidation thwarted;
As I put myself under my dome.

When my face was slapped;
I was pushed and bounced off the wall;
My last nerve should have been tapped;
Instead, I remained sore;
Silent as my consciousness lapsed.

As my way of escape;
I'd find myself a fantasy;
With unicorns, wizards and pink apes;
And anything else I'd fancy;
Like princes adorned in capes.

They'd be polite and gentle;
To the princess, that was I;
To this, my fantasy was central;
And reached to the sky;
To a height ever so tall.

And I was never weak;
I could defend myself;
I wielded a sword so sleek;
It was bad for my enemy's health;
A dragon, accompanied by a reek.

It often had my father's face;
But I didn't fight alone;
When we found it's hiding place;
For sins, it had to atone;
Without any elegance or grace.

These dreams were often cut short;
With a slam of my bedroom door;
My throat grew taut;
I didn't want anymore;
The underneath of my bed, I sought.

But it would be futile;
For all my efforts;
My ankles were snatched, in rough style;
No matter how I fought;
I was too small to do anything worthwhile.

He started another beating;
I couldn't stop this time;
Erupting into frantic bleating;
For someone to save his body of mine;
It didn't want defeating.

Mother came to my aid;
After the police had been called;
Our debt to him had been paid;
The ogre had momentarily been felled;
And our escape path had been laid.

Much changed after we had been freed;
All for the better;
No longer controlled by greed;
We lived to the letter;
Our life, he would no longer impede.

He served a short term;
But he wasn’t in prison;
For as long as he did deserve;
In my opinion.
Now we had cut ties with that worm;
I felt that I was in a safe union.

Changes

Enter my teenage years;
Where I was very difficult;
Picked fights with my peers;
Nothing magnificent;
Just biffed a few ears.

They blamed the lack of a father;
Though he taught me violence;
It was something larger;
The loss of my innocence;
Something I couldn't barter.

But that had already been discussed;
That wasn't the entirety;
My body had been brushed;
By a brand new identity;
That left my skin blushed.

I had hair in new places;
And bled on the regular;
Spots were on all our faces;
Some grew like a pillar;
Whilst others filled spaces.

I wanted to cry all the time;
And never knew why;
My shirt had a rising hemline;
Which made me sigh;
The breasts I'd grown, took no time.

I suddenly needed a new wardrobe;
After my expansion;
I seemed to be as big as a globe;
Too big to fit in even a mansion;
And uglier than a smashed gnome.

There was this new feeling too;
Something I just couldn't describe;
Many of the boys, I wished to woo;
Kiss them and take them for… A ride?
Scratch that, I didn't know what to do.

I was a whole muddle of emotions;
Feelings, desires and needs;
As though riding a locomotion;
Speeding through thick trees;
Causing untold commotion.

Mostly with my teachers;
For which I gained much punishment;
In which my tutors became preachers;
Where they were in their element;
Less human, more creatures.

In the mind of a fourteen year old;
Which was mostly negative;
To adults, I remained cold;
My behaviour, less than festive;
At least, so I am told.

I honestly didn't know why;
I behaved the way I did;
No-one saw eye-to-eye;
With myself, to be candid;
My behaviour wasn't going to fly.

I also went through phases;
Some weirder than others;
Horrific in some cases;
I definitely felt sorry for my mother;
A daughter of many faces.

I even remember my first kiss;
A bad boy with a lip ring;
Who smoked mostly cannabis;
Whilst copious lager was his thing;
Mostly, something was amiss.

Hormones did give me an excuse;
To behave irrationally;
And often obtuse.
I'm glad that time is behind me;

When my body suffered it's own abuse;
Moving forward was better, a certainty.

Broken, Until the Next Time

My heart pounded in my chest;
And my palms began to sweat;
You were the one I desired;
For whom all my passions fired;
I dared not show how I felt;
For I'd known the card I'd been dealt.

I was awkward and unattractive;
With an insecure mind so very active;
So when you called my name;
I knew life would never be the same;
The way you kissed me;
And the way you held me.

It set my heart on fire;
Flames grew faster than a funeral's pyre;
I was so sure you were the one;
The wedding planning was almost done;
Our children had been named;
Shortly before my heart was maimed.

I gazed into your eyes for hours;
When you gave me my first flowers;
I'd smile whenever I thought of you;
I hoped I made you happy too;

At least, for a little while;
Before you dumped me in style.

At least it was in person;
Not the mobile version;
Though, honestly, it didn't soften the blow;
It still made me really, really low;
There wasn't enough cake in the world;
To heal what had unfurled.

My face hurt from sobbing;
Red, raw and throbbing;
I was surrounded by soaked tissues;
I kept Kleenex in business with the amount I used;
I was crushed, broken, falling apart;
In fact, I made despair an art!

Our relationship was so much less than a dream;
It had swept me downstream;
Dragged into the depths;
The undercurrent taking my last breath;
Why could no-one see?
Did they not care what this did to me?

My skin was burning;
Stomach churning;
Throat raw and becoming tight;
Absolutely nothing felt right;

Mother told me to pull myself together;
I wasn't going to recover – ever!

Every bone was broken;
I was falling apart and choking;
My fingers gripped my pillow tight;
As I cried all night;
Once again, falling asleep in a pool of my tears;
And surrounded by my fears.

Would I ever find another lover;
Or was my dating life over?
Once I'd fallen into self-pity;
Could I form another entity.
For myself, before its too late?
Had I already locked the gate?

Men, who'd want one?
Though, they can be handsome;
So annoying, the only conclusion is to shoot;
But, they can be so cute;
That's it, I was going to stop;
Damn, they are so hot!
Dating – I wasn't going to miss;
Even when all I crave is a kiss;
Life was as sour as a lime;
So, I was broken, until the next time.

Climax or Anti-Climax?

My hands shook and fumbled;
Out of my mouth, stutters mumbled;
You silenced them with trembling lips;
Moans rumbled in my throat with a sway of my hips;
It seemed to make you excited;
A feeling that was requited.

You threw me on the bed;
Pulled my arms above my head;
Your kisses were rough, impetuous;
I was hoping for something adventurous;
Fingertips found their way under my clothes;
I gasped and shuddered – I needed more of those.

I slipped my tongue between your teeth;
As your hands ventured beneath;
And found their way between my legs;
I pressed my mouth against your ear to hear my begs;
I wanted you to strip me;
I imagined pleasure to infinity.

My body would shake;
My mouth agape;
Moans would fill the air;
With your hand in my underwear;
I might even say your name;
If you'd promise to pleasure me again.

That was my fantasy;
To feel uncontrollable ecstasy;
I knew my first time would be different;
But I was still expectant;
I still wanted to have fun;
Even if it wasn't expertly done.

You groans let me know;
That I was satisfying, so;
With my rhythmical hands;
Turning you into a sexy young man;
Which I wanted to feel within;
Honestly, I was desperate to begin.

With frantic fingers, I gripped;
And at your shirt, I ripped;
Babbling for your intimacy;
For you to feel me with intricacy;
Your hands shook and pulled at my flies;
At your touch, I closed my eyes.

My attire was yanked from my body;
You were set to put me to bed like hot toddy;
A nip on your lip closed the gap;
Slowly inside me, you were inserted;
A sharp gasp, I exerted.

The please I'd expected;
Was somewhat defective;
Instead, a pain sharp and pinching;
That caused nothing but wincing;
You did care for me so sweetly;
Even though I tried to complain discreetly.

Once you'd slowed down;
The sensation turned around;
My legs crossed over your back;
Your should with my nails, I did attack;
I gasped and groaned;
Against your body, hot and toned.

Just as it was getting good;
It seemed to end faster than it should;
'Was that it?' I asked;
Most certainly shorted than you were tasked;
You asked me if I'd finished;
My hope for more entirely diminished.

Aesop's Fables were put into place;
Slow and steady would have won that race;

Or perhaps it would have done nothing;
You certainly were no stud-muffin;
I wanted to tell you to go;
And take with you your false bravado.

I laid naked on my bed;
A hand placed on my head;
You looked at me and beamed;
It seemed so awfully obscene;
I decided to be honest;
And your skills I admonished.

I didn't want to take your confidence;
For me, it'd been a terrible experience;
You needed to last more than sixty-seconds;
Pointers definitely beckoned;
I was willing to show you where to touch;
You proclaimed you didn't fancy me much;
Our connection came to an end;
That night, it was just myself and my hand.

The Hole You Left

One of the days I feared the most arrived;
A time that truly tore my heart apart;
Seeing a man whom had once thrived;
Slowly and painfully depart;
Was something I thought I myself would not
survive.

My beloved Grandfather;
The man who cared for me;
More than any other;
Had left us spiritually;
His soul floated into the aether.

I sat in that chilled room;
And stared at the long, wooden box;
That was set to be his tomb;
It felt as though a paradox;
Had begun to loom.

How could a man such as he;
Have ever… Passed away?
He had been so alive, it was plain to see;
I never thought I'd see the day;
Where he ceased to be.

I continued to stare;
At his coffin, oak and polished;
Just waiting for him to give us a scare;
Our sorrows demolished;
As his lungs started to breathe the air.

He'd ask us why we were crying;;
And greet us with a smile;
He'd fallen asleep while in the coffin he was lying;
Only, he had been there for a while;
His consciousness seemingly defying.

He'd return to us entirely;
With all the jokes he could muster;
For he had been given immortality;
In copious and generous clusters;
He deserved nothing less than eternity.

Unfortunately, that was but a wish;
The coffin lid remained unmoved;
He had received life's final kiss;
So undeserved;
The magic in life, with him, had vanished.

My vision blurred;
As tears filled my eyes;
Silently, they escaped and rolled;

Down my cheeks to splash upon my thighs;
That stiff upper lip deterred.

The vicar spoke his words;
Written or him on paper sheet;
The endings of some slurred;
He himself ready to weep;
The line between professional and friend
blurred.

Honestly, he had been that for all;
A kind ear to lend, one to raise the mood;
With problems, upon him you'd call;
He'd never be harsh or rude;
His support was for the long haul.

We were asked to stand;
For a song all about him;
I clenched my tear-stained hands;
My eyes full to the brim;
On the inside, I felt nothing but bland.

In a state of confusion;
I looked towards the sun;
Soon would be the intrusion;
Of the sadness yet to come;
My grief reaching its conclusion.

As your coffin started to leave;
I still hoped against hope;
That you may somehow relieve;
This horrendous lump in my throat;
And raise yourself for all to see.

But it never happened;
It never came to pass;
My bottom lip stiffened;
My hope couldn't last;
The grief, it would not have lessened.

The events that followed were a blur;
Something my brain had not acquired;
I was sure they'd concur;
That our situation was dire;
For all of us who hurt.

You left a gaping hole;
In all our lives;
But, it was because of your important role;
That our love for you still thrives;
After all these years without your soul;
On Earth with us, cracking wise;
Everything seemed so very cold;

Saying all this, I was so happy I had known you;
In fact, I would say I was blessed;
It had been a long time, it's true;

But my love was strong, as you may have guessed;
And now – when I reminisce – I am not blue;
It helps me when I am stressed;
To imagine your advice, impromptu;
It made my heart yearn in my chest;
When I had pain only you could soothe;
Because, you truly were the best Grandfather I could have wished for.

Too Close for Comfort

My friend and I;
The one I'd befriended;
When I was young and shy;
With our schedules up-ended;
Had decided to run awry.

It was a dark night;
One of mystery and wonder;
Whilst we were dazzled by the light;
It seemed to be a spell we were under;
That falsely made us feel that the world was
right.

We both cackled loudly;
Obnoxiously so, I would have to say;
Hindsight would stop me from acting so boldly;
But I didn't think of such on that day;
I warmly enjoyed a night that would end coldly.

We swayed arm-in-arm;
Screaming out our joy;
We didn't see the harm;
In our playful ploy;
That we had coated in our charms.

We separated for a moment;
My friend fetching us drinks;
I was serene, relaxed and content;
I never stopped to think;
Someone would forego my consent;
And push me to the brink.

I continued to dance on my own;
Unaware that I was being approached;
By someone who had a heart of stone;
To whom I would feel reproach;
For sins he could never atone.

As I swayed my hips;
I was grabbed from behind;
A near silent scream escaped my lips;
For a moment, I was blind;
I couldn't see which way this would slip.

I tried to plant an elbow against his jaw;
Whilst he roughly groped my breast;
I was prepared to scream until my throat was raw;
But I couldn't decide what was best;
All I knew was that I was going to be sore.

I wanted to fight;
I honestly did;
But my thoughts took flight;

As I was consumed by fright.

His hands found my thighs;
His nails dug into my flesh;
I knew I had to be weary of guys;
Nothing more, nothing less;
Should I have just stayed home to hide?

It only got worse;
As I was forced into the wall to my left;
It seemed I was under a curse;
My face tear-streaked, pressed against paper,
bereft;
I feared I'd leave in a hearse.

He pulled at my clothes;
And, on the inside, I started to panic;
On the outside, I froze;
Whilst my brain went manic;
The absence of a yes can still be a no.

Just as I'd accepted my fate;
I started to feel something shift;
It was his weight;
An end to the violent tryst;
More accurately, a meeting of hate.

Someone had taken note;
Of my sudden assault;

My voice was just a gargle in my throat;
After it'd been brought to a halt;
I knew my insecurities would bloat;
Later, I'd be sure it was my fault.

My party companion returned;
Paler than a ghost;
Our night had been curtained;
A disappointment to most;
But my relief was sustained.

I wanted to run;
Find my way home;
And hide from the sun;
Locked in my comfort zone;
Safe, but solemn.

I knew that wouldn't be permanent;
I was told as such;
By the police Sergeant;
And the others in touch;
It would not set like cement;
Until later, by much.

It affected me for years;
Although it was kept underneath;
Often bringing me to tears;
And tearing me apart beneath;
It coming to the forefront was in my fears;

So I kept it tightly sheathed;
But from that, a better future surely nears.

A Cog in the Machine

I knew it was coming;
But I didn't resent it any less;
If I didn't want to be slumming;
I would have to join this job mess;
Through advertisements, I'd been thumbing.

After much defeat;
I was finally selected;
On a day filled with sleet;
From the job, I almost defected;
Purely because that was not so neat.

I did, instead, persevere;
Despite the appearance of a drowned rat;
I wasn't greeted with a sneer;
But neither a tip of the hat;
Just to make that clear.

I proceeded toward my boss;
Very reluctantly, I might add;
My Marxism had suffered a loss;
For this capitalist fad;
Which came at a cost.

It was only my first day;
An introduction, turn up and be seen;
But I had to say;
I felt like I was now part of the machine;
It made my gills turn grey.

My soon-to-be oppressor looked me in the eye;
Readying me for mundane torture;
Though I wouldn't let them see me cry;
I knew I had a battle in my future;
Because when the rich wage war, it's the poor
who die.

Perhaps I was being excessive;
My mother said it was a phase;
But I refused to be submissive;
I would not let my eyes glaze;
And of others' pain, be dismissive.

I would join a union;
As soon as my job was confirmed;
Turn my co-workers into a communion;
Make sure the bourgeois get burned;
Before my excommunication.

I took commands with gritted teeth;
I didn't like to be dictated to;
The revolution would come from beneath;
An all-out, unstoppable coup;

A fight that was beyond belief.

Though I would have to be careful;
Capitalism did have an overbearing power;
I would have to pretend to be grateful;
Even though forced labour made me sour;
My responses would have to remain tasteful.

There was so much paperwork to sign;
I stared at it with dismay;
There was disscontempt with each line;
I wrote in ink as I scratched my life away;
To be used as another piece in their mine.

It seemed so wrong right then;
For me to be partaking in something such as
that;
In fact, I'd say I was coerced to us a pen;
And to don their silly hat;
To do it again and again.

I was being told how to act;
How to speak and how to dress;
As though I had no tact;
It seemed patronising and meaningless;
Not an opinion, merely a fact.

I'd find a way to stand out;
To keep my individuality;

There would be rules I could flout;
Whilst sticking with the formality;
To appease anyone with clout.

The change from school was a shock;
The biggest after how much money controlled;
My anarchist manifesto life was harder to lock;
When your behaviour was thoroughly patrolled;
And more powers that have stock.

I didn't lat long in that job;
Not because of my attitude;
Or a decided snob;
There wasn't funds for fortitude;
No more cooking on their hob.

With time, I became complacent;
I'd been ground down by the gears;
Until working for hours made me content;
And I continued to do so for years;
Copious amounts of time ill spent;
Some of them left me in tears;
Until I found my happiness, Heaven sent.

It kept my joy palpable;
And made me feel complete;
Introduced me to humans most stable;
One with whom no other could compete;
But that was for another day, another fable;

Just the first of a fleet;
That would place them on such a table;
For now, I'll tidy that away in a box, nice and neat;
And easily retrieved with a thick cable.

In a Heartbeat

I didn't believe in love at first sight;
Something reserved for Fairytales;
For a romantic's fictional delight;
But then, in an instant;
I was nothing but contrite.

A pair of eyes met mine;
Full of life and laughter;
And – dare I say – divine?
Our surroundings blurred to nothing;
A scenario so asinine!

Their smile set my heart ablaze;
Whilst I became woozy;
Consumed by a favourable haze;
I felt myself return a grin;
Like one of a drunken daze.

I had never been a believer;
But, in that moment, I wondered;
Could science be the conceiver;
Of someone created just for me?
It must have been a divine weaver!

A being who created thee;
Produced nothing short of an angel;
Who was approaching… Me?

It seemed I was not sole and alone;
In this overwhelming glee.

I studied your face as you spoke;
Everything I could have dreamed of;
I just begged not to choke;
I knew then-and-there, somehow;
That you were, for me, bespoke.

You asked me for my name;
I was dumbstruck in your presence;
Befuddled, mute, shaken and lame;
How could you have looked upon me;
With anything but disdain?

But you laughed instead;
And introduced yourself;
Whilst a buzz consumed my head;
I mumbled the word I identified with;
As my legs turned to lead.

It's a wonder we had coffee;
As such an inadequate flirt;
Perhaps, if it had been left to me;
We'd have never moved;
Our first kiss remaining a fantasy.
A touch of your lips;
Sent a tingle through my spine;
The same when your hands caress my hips;
And venture between my thighs;
Reality and decorum slips.

The times we laughed;
Are the ones I love most;
Write it on my epitaph;
That your humour sustained my host;
Took my breath away until the very last.

Walk upon the beach;
And holidays in the snow;
Our hearts were no longer one for each;
Of us – there was just one heart in tow;
My half from you, and mine for you, my peach.

You were not just my love, but my best friend;
Someone who's time I treasured;
Whom I'd always defend;
Whom I loved more than could be measured;
And for whom my adoration would not bend.

Since that first day;
Our hearts have beat as one;
Life always seems to find a way;
To locate light where there was none;
With you, my soul shall lay;
Until my time is done.

The Bells

I was told this was a day;
That all women dreamed of;
I wondered who they surveyed;
Because a young me would scoff;
To think I'd do this, and change my name.

I knew of many who would criticise;
And they had every right;
For I had protested and demonised;
The act of wearing a dress so white;
Though mine was dark blue, to heathenise.

Mother-in-law wasn't happy;
About my colour choice;
I said white is virginal, quite snappy;
She soon lost her voice;
And looked like she wanted to get slappy.

My own was perplexed;
By my sudden change of heart;
She must've thought me hexed;
But I didn't know where to start;
My thoughts seemingly complex.

I hated to think that I'd submitted;
To the patriarchy;
My support to women intermitted;
When I said 'yes' to this wedding malarkey;
Is a feminist getting married permitted?

I wasn't sure how it had been decided;
And I couldn't pinpoint when;
I'm sure it coincided;
With when I met a Prince among men;
Though, was my opinion misguided?

I slumped into my seat;
Clutching at my dress' fabric;
Gasping from a new-found heat;
And sweating something tragic;
Was I about to admit defeat?

My mother gave me reassurance;
Jitters were normal;
The in-laws had endurance;
When giving me a scolding, so formal;
I started to feel that I needed life insurance!

It certainly didn't help my nerves;
Now, I really couldn't breathe;
In fact, it just made it worse;
Which was easy to perceive;
And was pushing me into reverse.

I felt I was going to cry and be dismissed;
But my makeup had only just been done;
Buy a professional stylist;
Hired by a particular crone;
Which made me realise, I must persist.

For the man I had given my heart to;
And to prove to his mother;
That I was good enough to pursue;
That he shouldn't have given his heart to another;
And our love would last until time was through.

I came to a revelation;
That I was fighting for all rights;
To work hard or enjoy relaxation;
To be safe during both days and nights;
To remain single, or to have relations.

Therefore, I was fighting for choice;
To be able to have one love, and not be forced;
So we could all have a voice;
Rather than be silenced and inert;
Clearly, I had made mine, I could rejoice.

Somewhere, deep within;
I found the courage I required;
To stand tall against the wind;
Place myself in the line of fire;

And ignore people's mithering.

I took a deep breath;
Stood to my feet;
And smoothed my dress;
To make sure it was neat;
After my distress.

As I grabbed my bouquet;
I knew my decision was correct;
I would have to answer, direct;
Allow them to revel in dismay.

After all, there was nothing more punk;
Than continuing your life without a care;
Whilst the others littered it with junk;
That, to me, was seemingly unfair;
After all, I was marrying a hunk!

Maybe I shouldn't have said that;
Considering my previous thoughts;
If I didn't like being sexualised by a rat;
Perhaps I shouldn't do so for the man I sought;
You know, tit-for-tat.

I shook those thoughts from my head;
As my heels clicked against concrete;
On my way to the aisle I was set to tread;
Towards the man I was set to meet;

Spend the rest of my life with, in joy or dread.

You spied me from the altar and smiled;
I couldn't help but respond equally;
And could have sworn I saw tears in your eyes;
Which you would shed gleefully;
Accompanied by deep, steadying sighs.

Once we were level;
I whispered that you were gorgeous;
A compliment in which I was sure you would revel;
But instead, a grin spread across your face, enormous;
Like that of a beautiful, cheeky devil.

When the vows were read;
My heart began to swell;
Until it was bigger than my head;
And I'd never felt so well;
I wanted to skip those words and kiss you instead.

I was glad I did not;
Because your lines were stunning;
Every syllable meant a lot;
If said from a distance, I'd have come running;
I watched you, lost in thought;
I felt as though I was basking, sunning;

In his brilliant prescience – better than you, there was nought.

I eagerly said ‘I do’;
Screamed it even;
So enthusiastic to marry you;
More than I’d have ever been believing;
You repeated my words my in tune;
All I knew in that moment was that I loved you.

The years we spent together;
Had their ups and downs;
But we were tougher than leather;
Whether with a smile or a frown;
On that day – and thereafter – you were my forever;
And the one who supported my crown;
I would be without you, never.

Somber and Delight

I sat on the lip of my bath;
Feeling more anxious than I'd ever done before;
The stick in my hand was brash;
As the lines started to solidify;
And tears formed on my bottom lash.

Once it all became clear;
A smile broke upon my lips;
I couldn't wait to yell into my husband's ear;
That we were going to be parents;
In a future relatively near.

I'm sure he cried more than I;
When I broke the news;
Though there wasn't a dry eye;
Between either of us two;
I was so happy, I felt like I could fly.

He held me close and declared his love;
For both myself and our unborn child;
His words sang to me like a dove;
As he caressed my barely swollen abdomen;
Seemingly regarding it as something from
above.

He littered my face with kisses;
Making me giggle and squirm;
However, my joy would change to be listless;
Once my world inevitably came crashing down;
In an explosive, blinding mist.

I lay in bed one night;
Warm, content and sound asleep;
Finally happy in the arms of my white knight;
When I was awakened by a searing pain;
In my stomach, so intense I started to cry.

Initially, I didn't know why;
I clutched the sheets and pulled them back;
To see the blood trickling down my thigh;
I hastily forced my spouse to awaken;
Which he did with sleepy eyes.

However, that soon changed;
As he wobbled to the car, shaken;
And also stirred by someone seemingly
deranged;
Screaming, panicking and demanding he move;
Tot take me to the hospital, post-haste.

There were so many emotion;
None of which I could express;
I'd found a new devotion;
And it had been ripped away;

So finally, I was left with devastation.

They had been lost;
Left a life they never had;
Though there was physical cost;
It was the emotional pain;
That cut the deepest, and hurt the most.

My partner held my hand;
Whilst I waited in the ward bed;
The IV bag hooked on a stand;
I silently stared into the distance;
Hoping to drift into a far-off land.

The doctors saw to me;
And I cried myself to sleep;
Once I was home, I was still weak and weary;
My lightheadedness made my knees collapse;
I sat on the floor, tired and empty.

I spread my news;
And was informed it was Sade;
The sympathy was few;
Which I'm sure was just my self-pity;
I needed to wallow in slew.

Though my child had been small;
And within me for such a short time;
I felt like I'd suffered a great fall;

But I kept that to myself;
They didn't wan to know it all.

When I became pregnant again;
I was hesitant to be joyous;
Last time, my happiness went down the drain;
We heat it between ourselves;
And waited until a later time frame.

Nine months passed;
The day finally arrived;
The hospital had me in bed, gassed;
As I pushed like my life depended on it;
I prayed to know how long it'd last.

I held my baby in my arms;
Still dripping in sweat;
I'm sure I bore no charm;
I gazed upon her tiny face;
And knew I'd protect her from all harm.

Yes, our baby was a girl;
Though I may be biased;
The prettiest in the whole world;
I knew then, I couldn't love her more;
For she was made of diamonds and pearls.

I knew she had been worth the wait;
The pain, the agony;

The sorrow and family disgrace;
Though I still felt love for the child, gone;
My love for her reached outer-space;
I'd do all I could to make her happy;
All opportunities, I'd open the gate;
There was absolutely nothing I wouldn't do;
To keep an eternal smile on her face.

Progeny

Now, our child, we adored;
She was a meld of ourselves and the person we loved;
But sometimes, her behaviour we abhorred;
When she tore about the house;
And the wallpaper, she tore.

There were so many ways;
That she reminded me of myself;
A rambunctious little tear away;
Who could not be tamed;
I just couldn't find the words to say.

It is both admirable and abhorrent;
When they are so headstrong;
On one hand, they can fight off even the fastest torrent;
But on the other;
To your discipline, they remain despondent.

And then there is the sarcasm;
For which you must scold them;
But how can you be the matriarchal madam;
When you yourself can't help but smirk;
At the words they have fashioned.

I had never thought that would create;
A mini-version of myself;
When wanting a shield, I did not hesitate;
Assuming that they would be a better person;
More kind, sweet and sedate.

But though I may sound disappointed;
Really, I am not;
A part of me feels anointed;
For the child that I have got;
She is perfect, her questions pointed;
She'd always known exactly what she wanted in life;
Even when she didn't have the words to coin it;
And for that, I was grateful;
That I had been blessed with a daughter who couldn't be taunted.

As a small child, it was cute;
When she knew something extra;
And informed adults of her knowledge pursuit;
But as she grew older, it became something else;
Often a verbal dispute;
Alongside banners and flags;
Walking down streets with videos they'd shoot;
Protesting the wrongs of the world;
No matter how minute.
Once again, I admired her spirit;
I could not deny that;

But I worried for her safety when she was in it;
Those crowds upon mass;
Fighting for against the oppressors, the idiots;
Who ran the world like lunatics;
Letting the rich get richer, while the poor just
have to deal with it;
When there is enough wealth for all;
Upon this rotating rock of ours, this lonely
planet.

I was so proud she had integrity;
Of that, I would not lie;
I just wished I knew she had safety;
When not under my watchful eye;
A pain well know to those with child of
flexibility;
As they age a need you to care for them less;
The brain is consumed with morbidity;
As you wonder if they knew, for them, what is
best;
With that, teenagers have rigidity.

I could have told until my face turned blue;
That I was not trying to patronise;
I still saw her as my child, it was true;
But that part of me would never die;
Even if I was still alive to see her at one-hundred
and two;
She'd still be my baby;

And I'd worry about every she might do.

Once they were off the tight parenting leash;
And making their own decisions;
It was so much that my control had found a new lease;
Just that I couldn't see the dangers around them;
So my brain created putrid images, both terrifying and niche;
That disturbed my head and twisted my stomach;
It caused me to be unable to sleep;
Once she had started university;
We felt like we'd drifted away, a friendship we just couldn't keep.

I know my husband thought it irrational;
For me to worry the way I did;
But he was always so casual;
As though there was nothing that could phase him;
Not even a catastrophe national.

He would soothe my worries with his words;
Try to reassure me that she was okay;
She was a strong girl;
And knew how to keep herself safe;
Even in this dangerous world.

He thought he meant well;
And he thought that he was right;
But I am afraid that men cannot tell;
Just how dangerous the world is;
When you are a woman considered small and fragile.

Men became the boogeyman around the corner;
As you walked home from a night shift;
A key between your fingers was in order;
If his footsteps became increasingly audible;
Narrowing the gap between you and a coroner.

They didn't seem to understand;
The threats that we faced every day;
Once I explained to him mine, firsthand;
His mind was changed there and then;
And his face was paler than Bondi sand.

Then it was his turn to panic worse than I;
And accuse all others of being evil;
Seemed to think every lock was sly;
Somehow medieval;
Like they were murderous guys.

He suddenly knew how we felt;
And was disgusted by it;
Creating armour in his smelt;
For a daughter more precious than anything;

Whilst simultaneously bearing a heart of guilt.

He'd been around women all his life;
His mother, sisters;
Cousins, and his beloved wife;
But he hadn't been able to see the true dangers;
Until shown – by his daughter – a woman's
strife.

As I said, I was so amazingly proud of her;
I just wished that she could have remained a
child;
For a whole while longer;
I have so many stories from her childhood to
tell;
There's just something about them that makes
me hunger;
For another baby, a friend for my sweet cherub;
We were never blessed with such a moniker;
As to be a four person family;
After we had tried many times together;
I just couldn't seem to conceive;
No matter how much I wanted another.

Our fate had been decided for us;
As I cried into my husband's shoulder;
My womb was barren, and caused a lot of fuss;
For myself and my doctors;
Once pain meds and operations became a must.

But I wish to forego such stories;
For they make me think of the things I could have had;
Whilst I should appreciate life's little glories;
And the love I have been given;
Rather than curse my malfunctioning ovaries.

Which is why the nest story I shall tell;
Goes back to a time when I learnt a lesson;
That I should have known all to well;
Before I let the emotion cloud me;
And from my important place inside a child's heart;
Her mother fell;
From upon the golden pedestal;
Deep down to the bottom of the well.

Repeat the Mistake

I clenched my hands into a fist;
Upon that night, I could not hold my temper;
I feared my partner may be in a tryst;
With a woman other than I;
Someone beautiful, a mysterious Miss.

My friends had heard whispers;
Oh so dire and besmirching;
They were known to be interfering listeners;
Of which I did not approve;
But they had become to me, sisters.

I awaited the door hinges creak;
When my husband would return;
For not a fight I did seek;
But the truth, and to face him;
Rather than be simply meek.

A jingle of his keys caught my ears;
And I strode from the lounge;
My stomach bubbled with anxious fears;
Once I saw his face filled with gloom;
Was he so miserable because I was near?

I began a confrontation;
With a reddened face;
Attacking without hesitation;
And a steady pace;
I forcefully started my investigation.

He was taken by surprise;
Especially by my aggressive stance;
But I was not going to be taken in by lies;
Though neither was I one to listen to gossip;
Despite the fact I had this time.

It was his turn to become flushed;
As he claimed I was preposterous;
How could I believe a fabrication so rushed;
When he had been so loyal through the worst;
Something in which a weaker marriage would've been crushed.

I screamed at the top of my lungs;
That his betrayal had broken me some;
I'd been climbing a ladder, and found the broken rung;
My happiness had grown so much;
But now I was distraught, like I was when I was young.

I needed his reassurance;
That he had not strayed from me;

But instead, I gained defiance;
As he continued to shout;
In a tone most fierce.

It was clear to see he was hurt;
But my words and actions;
But I couldn't stop being curt;
Because inside, I was breaking;
I feared myself and our child, he would desert.

Perhaps she was a beautiful blonde;
A mystical temptress;
With legs so very long;
That she spread with ease;
Whenever he knew I was gone.

I couldn't allow myself to think such things;
It made me feel sick to my stomach;
And tied it up with strings;
And held me hostage;
After it had clipped my wings.

He tried his best to grab my hand;
Which I jerked away with haste;
Much sharper than I had planned;
I managed to deeply scratch his arm in the process;
Drops of blood on the floor, they did land.

I blamed him for his pain;
Though my accusation was unfounded;
I continued to glare with disdain;
He had neither confirmed nor denied;
A yes or no would have been better, stated plain.

He just looked at me, an expression of horror;
Mine was contorted;
Lips ready to snarl and my brows set to furrow;
His bloodied hands held his injury;
Whilst my patience grew lower.

There was a tiny squeak from the hall;
Of a started child;
She stared at us both, so scared and small;
It made my heart sink;
To see her love for us take a horrible fall.

In that moment, she was once again a mirror;
A mirror of myself;
When I myself was a minor;
Watching my father attack my mother;
Though, for him, it wasn't in an accidental manner.

There was many a night when I'd hear her screams;
Hide my face in my hands;
As I cried tears in streams;

Begged for him to stop hitting her;
To stop being so mean.

Hospital visits were the norm;
Broken ribs, a broken legs;
Very often, a broken arm;
Sometimes, it would be me;
Mostly concussions caused me harm.

The number I had as a child;
Should have damaged me irreparably;
Perhaps that was why I was so wild;
Somewhere amongst those injuries;
I had been rewired.

Perhaps that was why I struggled;
To offer my mother comfort;
With her, I never snuggled;
Just locked myself away within;
A world in which I was smuggled.

My daughter's tears started to form a lake;
Upon her cheeks and over her face;
Watching this was more than I could take;
I had to hold her tight;
I couldn't repeat my mistake.

She needed my reassurance immediately;
I couldn't let her think of me like that;

Her father had been hurt accidentally;
Though, through a child's eyes;
It may have been seen differently;
She needed my explanation;
A return of my reliability.

As I held her close to my chest;
I turned back to my husband;
A man whom I had always considered the best;
But on that day, had thought the worst;
And accused him of something I'd detest.

Apologies were given;
Cuddles were abundant;
In my daughter's eyes, I was forgiven;
Though my husband wasn't so cool;
It seemed for him, it would have to be written;
I was reassured by his story;
A visitor in town, in the form of his cousin;
Something I had been told before;
A link in my memories that I had been missing.

I'd managed to get myself lost in an
unfathomable fib;
Spread to me by gossiping girls;
With words so terribly glib;
I felt so stupid for believing them;
As they babbled and drooled onto their bibs.

I cleaned my partner's scrape;
And bandaged it the best I could;
A flurry of worry's came all too late;
Along with a stream of kisses, that I hoped he understood;
Meant I didn't want my fate;
To be life without him in my life;
For I would love him until my death date.

He held me tight and sighed;
For I now was the child;
And in him, I could confide;
He understood the reassurance I needed;
Due to the trauma I tried to hide.

The night drew in as we conversed;
A multitude of truths came out;
For better or for worse;
It ended with kisses and caresses;
So perfect, they seemed rehearsed;
Each other's bodies we cradled;
And our pain, we nursed.

The Empty Nest

A parent knows that eventually;
There child shall become an adult;
It always arrives painfully;
Sudden, without warning;
Something you can never prepare for dutifully.

It seems that time passes too fast;
One moment, they are a babe swaddled;
The next, their school day is their last;
The hands on the clock raced by;
In this film they had been cast.

A youthful, cheeky sprog;
Whom played with dolls and tea sets;
Could soon sprout into a moody goth;
Who insisted it was 'not a phase';
Before returning to a 'normal' cloth.

They started off learning letters;
Numbers and colours;
Suddenly, they were amongst your betters;
Learning complicated formulas and theorems;
And becoming academic trendsetters.

One day you were teaching them;

And suddenly, they seem to know more than
you;
In everything, English, French, Maths and
Chem.;
Or perhaps is was just that they thought they did;
And you remembered all that stuff when you
were as young as them.

But, the day had come;
Not finally, not eventually, but all too soon;
When our child would leave the home;
Pack up their belongs and go;
To find a place all their own.

We gathered everything in boxes;
And carried them to the vans;
We were silent as creeping foxes;
With very little to say, but so much to think;
One of those paradoxes.

As the last one was placed;
A tear formed in my eye;
A day I knew much be faced;
But I didn't want to say goodbye;
And had hoped would be more slowly paced.

My child turned and gave me a look;
With adult eyes;
Something I unwillingly took;

The acceptance of the passing of time;
As thought turning the pages of a book.

She said she would miss us;
But not as much as I;
As though she would go on a journey most perilous;
Adventuring with the Sultan of Brunei;
One that could only end disastrous.

I threw my arms around her;
And held her tight;
I wanted to remain the protector;
But if she were to go too far;
I feared I'd become nothing but the neglector.

She was so very startled;
But hugged me all the same;
Our eyes with tears, sparkled;
Perhaps hers more than mine;
And in our love for each other, we marvelled.

She insisted she'd stay in touch;
And I insisted she did;
For I loved her so much;
I couldn't bear to think of us becoming distant;
Onto my contact to her, I would clutch.

Her father wasn't so emotional;
As either she or I;
I knew he wouldn't let her see him cry at all;
But I knew that he would;
As soon as she pulled away, and was to far for us to call.

We held each other, my husband and I;
As we watched her leave;
And her car pull out of the drive;
As predicted, his face became wet;
As he waved with watery eyes.

The house wasn't going to be right;
Without our daughter around;
The girl who made it so bright;
It was so dreadfully quiet;
As though it were constantly the dead of night.

At least I did have some company;
And my husband and I were friends;
Or else, it would have been so lonely;
A time of misery without end;
Though it didn't make the building anymore homely.

I'd sit at the table and wait;
Wait for the phone to ring;

The time between became more than I could take;
As my stomach griped with anxiety;
I always felt her calls were late;
Finally, I heard the shrill tone;
And lifted the receiver to my face;
We'd end up chatting for hours;
Whilst I consumed slices of cake;
I refused to stop either;
Until there were merely crumbs upon my plate.

My Child's Child

My daughter and I spoke often;
But mostly on the phone;
Upon one day, her voice did soften;
To that of a merry, content tone;
I'd never heard her so softly spoken.

She informed me she'd found a partner;
Whom she loved and held dear;
I insisted she bring them home to myself and father;
For which she gladly obliged;
And the distance for us, she did charter.

We'd prepared something for them;
A very special dinner;
Something than we prepared for most men;
But I was so excited for the meeting;
I would have considered singing an anthem.

If this person made my child happy;
Then they did the same for me;
As long as they weren't snappy;
And caused her mind to befuddle;
The layer of love and joy that covered misery.

Once we eventually met;
I knew I had not need to worry;
Though I wouldn't have known that yet;
When I made my first assumptions;
He was the ideal gentleman, I'd have bet.

I could see the love in their eyes;
And I knew that it was genuine;
Neither was it felt by only one side;
It was all consuming for them both;
A wild wave on which they both did ride.

I shared a look with my husband;
As we both could see;
Though initially to believe, we were stubborn;
But she had most certainly given her heart to another;
Our daughter had found herself in a love-filled land.

We continued to meet many times;
All for separate occasions;
It was not a shock for us to find;
That one of the next was their engagement;
For it had lingered in my mind.

The wedding came too fast;
Only for my liking;
But I hoped it would last;

For my daughter's happiness was paramount;
Her life should have always been a blast.

But it still upset me in my gut;
To see her have grown so much;
As, down the aisle, she did strut;
I could see was an independent woman;
And herself, she could easily conduct.

It made me proud;
To know that I had raised her;
With the help of the man now silent when
normally loud;
Arm-in-arm with her and wearing a smile;
Her ambition, none could cloud.

My husband and I did discuss;
The amount that we did love;
The young couple for whom the day was to fuss;
We were overjoyed that our family was growing;
And couldn't wait for there to be more of us.

A wish that came true soon;
Announced to us with a swollen belly;
In truth, we were over the moon;
To know she we having a child;
But were not old enough to be grandparents so
soon!

It made us feel old and decrepit;
I started to count the greys;
My back did pop when I chose to sit;
My energy wasn't what it used to be;
But I couldn't be old, my life still had so much left of it.

I knew that my worries were somewhat vain;
For I knew of others whom had been far younger;
When they had joined the grandparent train;
Perhaps it was just a sign;
That I couldn't believe my child was an adult, again.

I helped her the best I could;
Offered her tips on how best to look after herself;
And the baby in the ways she should;
Some of it probably seemed unneeded;
But eventually, she would.

Time passed too quickly and too slow;
Somehow simultaneously;
I don't know how that could have been so;
She seemed to be pregnant forever;
But then, it was suddenly time for the bump to go.

After hours of painful labour;
We were informed they had been born;
A child in everyone's favour;
They'd had a son;
Named after their beloved neighbour.

Our child had to remain on the ward;
Due to complications;
But her child was anything but bored;
He wriggled and giggled in his cot;
And when he slept, he contently snored.

When I held him in my arms, gently cradled;
I carefully studied his face;
He was not the split genetics that was fabled;
I saw more of my daughter than her husband;
But her dead-ringer, he could not be labelled.

There were elements of his dad;
And of his paternal grandfather;
Though his eyes, those I had;
He had my husband's hair;
And of that, I was glad.

The same way I had with my own;
I fell in love with him instantly;
Once I touched him, the seeds of love were
sewn;
As I looked at him with tear-blurred vision;

He appeared to be glowing.

As though he were some supernatural creature;
Perhaps my angel had bore her own;
And perfect was every feature;
In those seconds, my love for him had grown;
Only once before had I performed this strange procedure.

The love for another is always different;
Depending upon who they are;
My love for my child was omnipotent;
Only ending upon my death;
Of that, I was more than confident;
And now, I felt this had spread to their child;
For them, I'd never be despondent.

I continued to cradle him;
Until my daughter fell asleep;
Her partner followed after a gap quite slim;
I smiled as they both snored contently;
I turned to my husband, but the sandman had also captured him.

I couldn't help but chuckle at the sight;
I could certainly see the family resemblance;
Between everyone else that night.

Twilight Beckons

My grandchildren were tearing about;
Making me grin and cackle;
Their enthusiasm, I wouldn't flout;
I stood to my feet to join in their fun;
But instead, started to feel down and out.

My feet slipped out from beneath;
There seemed to be a problem with my legs;
I fell down and clung to my seat;
Whilst I had a buzzing within my head;
Perhaps I was suffering from the heat?

The eldest came running to my aid;
As it tried to walk, and failed again;
The ground felt like water I had to wade;
That's when my chest began to tighten;
The pain was more than I could take.

I could hear some yelling;
Though I didn't know who;
Which I think was rather telling;
Of what I was going through;
And for others, it was apparently compelling.

My vision started to darken;
As the pain in my chest increased;
It was fading to black, became fuzzy rather than sharpened;
I tried my best to call for help;
But voice had already softened;
To nothing but a whisper.

I awakened some time later;
In a hospital bed, with drips in my arm;
And a taste at the back of my throat, so bitter;
Wires connected to machines;
That beeped for no other reason than to alarm.

Everything was blinding;
The white walls, the startling floor;
I'd wished it was darker, and cursed my timing;
I made an attempt to shout;
But my mouth was so dry, I just started miming.

A straw appeared, along with a small cup;
Out the corner of my eye;
Though really, it was nothing more than a sup;
Or a sip, it really was a tiny amount;
It would have all gone in one mouthful if I'd gone bottoms-up!

Though, I was in fact thankful for the straw;
As I could only consume tiny amounts;

Due to the fact my throat was raw;
The cup was held by my husband;
Who seemed to dislike what he saw.

As the ward lacked in a mirror;
I couldn't see how awful I looked;
I suppose if I could, it would have made my understanding clearer;
As to why he looked so weak due to my visage;
I just wished he could have tried to be cheerier.

He continued to stare in silence;
Whilst he helped the quench my thirst;
Under a nurse's guidance;
Whom I had not been aware of before;
For in my concentration, there had been some subsidence.

They didn't seem to know how to be polite;
As they forcefully grabbed my arm;
With a touch the opposite of light;
As they checked my blood-pressure;
And commented on how I had slept all night.

I was still relatively groggy;
So mustering a response was hard;
Especially with a brain so foggy;

As to the sequences of events that had sent me to hospital;
And forced me to skip the waiting lobby.

The doctor suddenly appeared, as though an apparition;
He started to tell me a series of events about myself;
But otherwise, there seemed to be no explanation;
At least, not as to what any of what he said meant;
He should've passed me a dictionary to find the words' definitions.

Whilst I didn't understand the Latin;
I understood the tone;
Neither myself or my family, it would gladden;
It was certainly possessive of a morbidity;
Most certainly something that would sadden.

I turned to my husband and sighed;
Whilst he grew even paler than before;
I didn't think I could comfort him if I tried;
A part of me started to worry about him;
And how he'd cope if I died.

Which is exactly what the doctor said;
Would happen to me;

In the coming months ahead;
Six months or twelve;
It didn't matter, it still filled me with dread.

My grandchildren were so young;
I thought I'd see the youngest grow some more;
I knew that I wouldn't be on the Earth for long;
But I just had thought it would be so short;
I wanted to do some more with my life before I was gone.

The news hadn't really settled in;
By the time I was discharged;
Once my brain processed it, I heard nothing but a din;
That blocked anything nice I might have heard;
Comfort for me becoming inert from within.

I had bottles of pills, blisters of tablets;
I'd have to taken them regularly to ease my symptoms;
As though I was drawn to them like magnets;
But they made me tired, and they were greatly disliked;
They made me remain mostly upon my mattress.

My husband did his best, to comfort;
My daughter and her partner to understand;

But their happiness – to me – should have
always come first;
I tried my best to hide my pain;
To it's maniacal hold, I refused to submit;
I would do my best to prolong the inevitable, for
their sake;
Though I knew, in this battle, I would never be
triumphant;
I'd climb this mountain and fight back;
Until I finally reached the summit;
My mother would have been proud;
That with my illness, I had not been
encompassed;
I vowed to make the most of my life, and spend
time with my family;
Right up until the point when my body would
dissolve into nothing but dust.

The Final Act

I am sitting in my rocking chair;
Looking to the sky;
It's strange, the memories you recall;
When you think you're going to die;
When you are caught in the Devil's snare.

I consider it strange;
The memories that had come to me;
Some of which I witnessed seemed deranged;
I previously would have not thought them important;
But clearly, my psyche did not feel the same.

Instead of all my career achievements;
Something that society says gives you worth;
I saw only the things money can't buy;
The love from my family, the sorrow of their loss;
Everything that – to me – was fundament.

When I boiled everything down;
To what was important to me;
The only thing I wanted was for my love to be grown;
A cultured by my friends and family;

In a world all of our own.

The sun is no less bright;
As it glares down upon me;
In fact, I seem to have an intensity of sight;
To view my final moments with superior clarity;
So I could take them with me, as some for of passage rite.

I'm looking at the age spots on my hand;
They seem to dazzle me;
Wherever the light lands;
My husband reaches for me from the chair to my left;
He seems blurry, and I utter words that he cannot understand.

I can feel my heartbeat slow;
And my eyelids are becoming heavy;
My hourglass is running low;
I turn my head to look at my husband's face;
As he gains an ethereal glow.

I cannot tell him I love him;
I just hope he already knows;
I'm getting weaker as my time grows slim;
My grip on his hand loosened upon his fingers;
Everything is growing dim.

I want to cling onto him forever;
I never want to let go;
I had accepted I would pass on into the never;
Though now I feel myself slipping away;
I was more scared than ever.

Thoughts are crossing my mind;
About where I might go next;
I don't really have the time;
To fully analyse something so complex;
But the coming future was mine.

Would I end up in Heaven?
With the bearded man and the pearly gates;
Or would I end up in one of the circles
numbered up to nine?
I am sure I have been bad in my life;
But is that enough to be labelled as sin?

There were so many other realms I might
eventually call home;
Gehenna, Nirvana, or return to the beginning of
Samsara;
Valhalla, Niflhel or Svartalfheim?
I suppose I am about to find out;
I am going from sighted to blind;
I think my heart has stopped;
This is the end;
This is my time.

The winged chariot has come for me;
The reaper wields his scythe;
The threads for me has been cut;
And the Ferryman, I have paid, for my life.

www.ingramcontent.com/pod-product-compliance
Lightning Source LLC
Chambersburg PA
CBHW051733130826
49812CB00033B/843
9789357213431